Positive Behavior for Everyone

By Amy R. Murray, M.Ed.

Grades K-5

© 2012 by YouthLight, Inc. | Chapin, SC 29036

All rights reserved. Permission is given for individuals to reproduce the worksheets in this book. Reproduction of any other material is strictly prohibited.

Layout and Design by Melody Taylor
Classroom Misbehavior Illustrations by Dan Kovasckitz.
Project Editing by Susan Bowman

Library of Congress Control Number
2011940948
ISBN
9781598501094

10 9 8 7 6 5 4 3 2 1
Printed in the United States

Table of Contents

About the Author 4
Dedication/Acknowledgements 5

Behavior Affects Everyone!
Introduction 6
Why you need this book 7

Section 1 - Positive Behavior Basics
Understanding Behavior 9
Q-TIP 10
Our First and Most Natural Response 10
The 4 Goals of Misbehavior 11
Attention 12
Power 18
Revenge 24
Display of Inadequacy 30

Section 2 - Communicating Positively
Verbalize the Good 37
Ineffective Teacher Language 38
Effective Teacher Language 39
Ineffective Parent Language 40
Effective Parent Language 41
Positive Discipline Works for Parents 42

Section 3 - A School-wide Plan for Teaching Behavior
School-wide Expectations 43
A SOAR Rule 44
SOAR Rule chart 46
Reproducible Classroom Posters 48
School-wide Lesson Plans 61
SOARing with Teacher Encouragement 69
School-wide Rewards 70
SOAR Cheer 74

Section 4: Classroom Activities & Lessons

Morning Meetings 75
Positive Ways to Greet..76
Celebrate Success 77
Let's SOAR Together 78
You Deserve a Trophy 85
Let's Juggle Together 87
Let's Keep Rolling...90
SOAR & More 92
To Tell or Not to Tell 94
I'm In a Pickle 96
Respect is the Key 99
Don't Break the Chain..101
Yes, I Can..103

Section 5: Small Group Activities & Lessons

You are Lucky 106
Safety Always 107
Happy Being Organized...108
Hands Up for Achievement...111
R is for Respect...113
Teasing Isn't Cool 114
I'm Angry 116
Let Go of Hurt 119
Good Behavior = Great Friends 121
Behavior to Flip Over 123

Section 6: Interventions for Challenging Students

Interventions..126
Cool Down Corner 127
Bitter to Sweet 130
Individualized Behavior Plans...131
Behavior Plans for Home 142

Resources & References..145

About the Author

✳ **Amy Murray** is a recently retired elementary school counselor from Dorchester District Two in Summerville, South Carolina. She worked for twenty-seven years in the school system as both an elementary school teacher and counselor. For the past twenty years, Amy worked as a school counselor at Windsor Hill Arts Infused Elementary School. Amy earned her B.A. degree in elementary education from Clemson University, and her M.Ed. degree in elementary counseling from The Citadel.

Positive Behavior for Everyone is Amy's fifth publication. She previously published three books through the National Center for Youth Issues: *Perfect Pals: How to Juggle Your Way From Perfection to Excellence, The Character & Career Connection,* and *Mending Hearts When a School Grieves. Hope for a Better Life,* Amy's first fiction book, based partly on her experiences as an adopted child, is available through www.lulu.com and www.amazon.com.

Dedication:
To all the students at
Windsor Hill Arts Infused Elementary School
I love you all and have learned so much from you!

Acknowledgements:
With special thanks to Bob & Susan Bowman
and all the great people at Youthlight, Inc.

Behavior Affects Everyone!

✳ Introduction

As an elementary school teacher and counselor for a combined twenty-seven years of experience, I realize now that I learned many things about helping students become successful through trial and error. This book was born out of a sincere desire to help educators learn how to empower students to perform their best academically every school day.

When I began my teaching career in 1979, I expected students to cooperate and follow my instructions. Most of the students were compliant, but I had little clue as to what to do when students refused to obey. I observed that behaviorally challenging students had other problems such as uninvolved or uneducated parents, a lack of desire to learn, or had experienced a trauma. I knew that if these misbehaving students didn't receive help, their academic progress would continue to be affected by poor behavior and they would lag behind others. I decided after a few years of teaching to earn a Master's degree in school counseling, as I wanted to help students reach their full potential for learning and success in life.

As a school counselor, I began to realize more and more that while I was successful in helping students perform better in classrooms after counseling and extra support, some students were continuing to misbehave. I learned that much of the student's misbehavior was due to the classroom environment. For years I had taught parents about the "Goals of Misbehavior" using the Systematic Training for Effective Parenting program, developed by Dinkmeyer, McKay, and Dinkmeyer. Now I realized teachers needed this information as well. I learned about PBIS—Positive Behavioral Interventions & Supports.* My focus as a counselor slowly shifted into more of a role as a behavioral interventionist; helping teachers to first teach positive behavior to their students and then helping them encourage students to maintain that positive behavior.

Amy R. Murray
*Developed by Dr. George Sugai and Robert Horner.

Why you need this book!

The most recent report from The National Center for Education Statistics (NCES) found that 46% of schools reported at least one student threat of physical attack during school year 2009-10. Some 10% of city schools reported at least one gang-related crime. There is no doubt that unruly behavior is increasing in our schools and becoming more violent.

If you are an educator or parent you are aware that children misbehave. The behavior children choose affects everyone around them. Learning cannot take place in a classroom when misbehavior is occurring! Learning is impaired not only for the disruptive student, but for everyone in the classroom!

A recent report from the National Center for Education Evaluation states: "We recommend that teachers actively teach students socially- and behaviorally-appropriate skills to replace problem behaviors using strategies focused on both individual students and the whole classroom. In doing so, teachers help students with behavior problems learn how, when, and where to use these new skills; increase the opportunities that the students have to exhibit appropriate behaviors; preserve a positive classroom climate; and manage consequences to reinforce students' display of positive replacement behaviors and adaptive skills."

Positive Behavior for Everyone contains all the information you need to actively teach children appropriate behavioral skills school-wide, in the classroom, and in the home. This book helps all educators and parents learn how to teach children positive behavior and how to motivate children to continue making positive behavior choices. This book helps you understand why children sometimes choose misbehavior. It explains how you can encourage positive behavior by simply changing the way you respond to misbehavior. This book also contains school-wide plans for teaching and promoting positive behavior, lessons for teachers, small group guidance sessions for counselors, and additional interventions for those extremely difficult students.

Positive Behavior for Everyone is a necessary resource book for those who work with children! It gives practical and easy to understand behavioral information for educators and parents divided into a user friendly format.

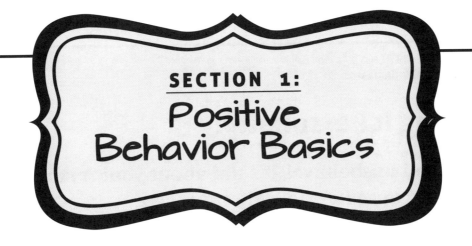

SECTION 1: Positive Behavior Basics

Understanding Behavior

It's simpler than you might first think. Ask yourself, "Why do you behave the way you do?" Behavior is chosen in our effort to contribute in a social situation. When you feel noticed and important in a social situation, good behavior choices are easy. When people notice you, compliment you, and expect good from you, you are motivated to demonstrate positive behavior. It is the same for children. I challenge you to form relationships with children and to find the good in every child.

Behavior has to be taught in our schools. Many children are not taught appropriate behavior in their homes. Many homes have no rules. While this may be frustrating for teachers, teaching cannot take place in a classroom without rules or in a classroom where disruptive behavior occurs. I promise you that if you take time to teach and reinforce rules both at the beginning of a school year and with reminders throughout the year, your classroom will have an atmosphere of mutual respect where learning can, and does, take place.

Disruptive students who come to you without structure and rules in their home can learn to be worthwhile, productive citizens in your classroom. A young teacher reminded me of this recently. She had two very disruptive students in her first grade classroom at the beginning of the school year. By forming relationships with them, teaching appropriate behavior expectations, and offering many rewards (both verbal and tangible) they became the best behaved students in her classroom! A teacher who focuses on teaching behavior expectations and rewarding positive behavior will create a respectful community of learners where all are successful!

{SECTION 1: POSITIVE BEHAVIOR BASICS}

Quit Taking It Personally!

When a student misbehaves it's not about you! A student misbehaves because he/she is discouraged.

The student needs you to give **encouragement.**

The student needs you to show **firmness and kindness.**

✱ **Our First and Most Natural Response to a Child's Inappropriate Behavior is Usually the Wrong One.**

- Usually creates more oppositional behavior
- Usually reinforces that inappropriate behavior
- MANY students need more instruction on behavior in the classroom, the same way some students need more instruction in academics.

{SECTION 1: POSITIVE BEHAVIOR BASICS}

The Four Goals of Misbehavior

Understanding the goals of misbehavior is critical to encourage positive behavior in a classroom!

Once you gain understanding in why students are making certain behavioral choices, you can learn how to respond to the misbehavior in a way that discourages it.

Attention
Power
Revenge
Display of Inadequacy

✱ **The Four Goals of Misbehavior was developed through the study of social behavior by Rudolph Dreikurs, social psychologist.**

{SECTION 1: POSITIVE BEHAVIOR BASICS}

Attention

Attention is definitely something we all yearn for. Can you imagine a day without attention from others? It is certainly no surprise that children need attention too! If children cannot get meaningful attention from adults, they will demand attention through acting out. Consider the following to recognize whether or not a child is seeking attention in negative ways.

How do I feel when the child misbehaves?
Annoyed or aggravated

How do I respond to the misbehavior?
Reminding or coaxing the child to do what is right

What is the child's response?
Stops the misbehavior temporarily

What does the child really need?

The child needs to be noticed! Unfortunately if you usually give attention to the child when he/she is misbehaving; you are encouraging the misbehavior to continue! Instead, ignore the misbehavior when it is a bid for your attention. Realize that the child needs your attention in positive ways. Compliment and call on the student when he/she is demonstrating positive behavior. A teacher can make time to talk with that student at lunch or recess. A teacher can give that student a classroom job. Students needing extra attention love to help other students and teachers.

{SECTION 1: POSITIVE BEHAVIOR BASICS}

Attention – Incorrect Response

When a teacher asks a student to quit an annoying behavior, the behavior may stop for a short while. Later the student will repeat the misbehavior because he/she received the wanted attention.

{SECTION 1: POSITIVE BEHAVIOR BASICS}

Attention – Correct Response

The teacher effectively changed the student's behavior by ignoring the inappropriate behavior and acknowledging the behavior she wanted. The student learned the best way to receive attention in class is by following the teacher's directions.

{SECTION 1: POSITIVE BEHAVIOR BASICS}

Attention – Incorrect Response

When a teacher asks a student to quit an annoying behavior, the behavior may stop for a short while. Later the student will repeat the misbehavior because he/she received the wanted attention.

{SECTION 1: POSITIVE BEHAVIOR BASICS}

Attention – Correct Response

The teacher could not ignore the misbehavior as it was interrupting instruction. The teacher chose to give the student a quiet reminder while offering a way the student could get the wanted attention by complying. The student learned the best way to receive attention in class is by following the teacher's directions.

(SECTION 1: POSITIVE BEHAVIOR BASICS)

Attention Seeking

✻ **All people, especially children, need attention!**

Ways to give positive attention:
- ✓ Compliments
- ✓ Noticing strengths
- ✓ Classroom jobs
- ✓ Happy Grams
- ✓ Good News phone calls
- ✓ Lunch with teacher
- ✓ Pats on the back

Don't!
- ✗ Show annoyance
- ✗ Coax
- ✗ Remind
- ✗ Punish

Remember

When students get attention in positive ways, they usually do not seek to belong through misbehavior.

(SECTION 1: POSITIVE BEHAVIOR BASICS)

Power

Everyone needs to have some power and control. Can you imagine a day without being given choices? We want children to learn to make good decisions. We must allow children to make some choices, even from a very young age, for them to develop decision-making skills. If children are not given the opportunity to choose, they may seek power through misbehavior. Consider the following to recognize whether or not a child is seeking power.

How do I feel when the child misbehaves?
Angry or threatened

How do I respond to the misbehavior?
Punishing or giving in

What is the child's response?
Defiant compliance; misbehavior intensifies

What does the child really need?

The child needs for you to stay out of conflict with him/her. Communicate that you understand you can't make him/her do something. Encourage the child to help you complete tasks. Give the child the ability to choose while realizing you, as the adult, control the choices. One example could be, "You can finish your work now, or complete it during recess." A routine class schedule helps students comply without a bid for power. Recognize your authority as a teacher—be kind and firm at the same time!

Power – Incorrect Response

When a teacher feels angry and demands compliance, the student's misbehavior usually intensifies. The student learns the teacher will argue with him/her.

{SECTION 1: POSITIVE BEHAVIOR BASICS}

Power – Correct Response

The teacher is frustrated with the student, but chose to stay calm and encourage the student to comply by giving choices. The student learned the importance of following directions to receive a privilege.

{SECTION 1: POSITIVE BEHAVIOR BASICS}

Power – Incorrect Response

When a teacher feels angry and demands compliance, the student's misbehavior usually intensifies. The teacher has unintentionally encouraged a power struggle.

{SECTION 1: POSITIVE BEHAVIOR BASICS}

Power – Correct Response

The teacher is frustrated with the student, but chose to stay calm and encourage by giving a compliment for compliance. The teacher is communicating to the students she cannot force compliance but cares about their feelings.

{SECTION 1: POSITIVE BEHAVIOR BASICS}

Power Seeking

✱ **All people, especially children, make decisions!**

Ways to give positive power:
- ✓ Communicate you can't make them
- ✓ Encourage task completion
- ✓ Offer to help
- ✓ Give choices
- ✓ Encourage decision making
- ✓ Recognize strengths

Don't!
- ✗ Stay in the conflict
- ✗ Display anger
- ✗ Give in
- ✗ Punish
- ✗ Threaten

Remember

When students start a power struggle, no one wins! By allowing students to make lots of choices, power struggles can be avoided.

{SECTION 1: POSITIVE BEHAVIOR BASICS}

Revenge

Revenge is an emotional response when someone has been deeply hurt. Have you ever felt revengeful? It is a terrible way for adults to feel. Children who feel revengeful and angry are close to spiraling out of control. Sometimes if children are not given any choices or power, they may seek revenge on adults. Consider the following to recognize whether or not a child is seeking revenge.

How do I feel when the child misbehaves?
Disappointed or hurt

How do I respond to the misbehavior?
Retaliating or getting even

What is the child's response?
Behavior escalates to get even or hurt back

What does the child really need?

The child needs for you to attempt to understand his/her feelings. Do not take the student's misbehavior personally. A child seeking revenge is hurting deeply, and needs an adult to listen and understand. For teachers this means scheduling a private time to listen to the student. You can demonstrate you care about the student's feelings without accepting the student's misbehavior. Try to build a strong relationship with the student.

The child needs for you to attempt to understand his/her feelings.

{SECTION 1: POSITIVE BEHAVIOR BASICS}

Revenge – Incorrect Response

When a teacher feels very angry and retaliates, the student's misbehavior usually escalates to get even with the teacher.

{SECTION 1: POSITIVE BEHAVIOR BASICS}

Revenge – Correct Response

The teacher is very angry with the student, but chose to stay cool and talk to the student in private. The teacher did not take the misbehavior personally and acknowledged the student's feelings. The student learned his teacher cares about him.

Revenge – Incorrect Response

When a teacher feels very angry and retaliates, the student's misbehavior usually escalates to get even with the teacher.

{SECTION 1: POSITIVE BEHAVIOR BASICS}

Revenge – Correct Response

The teacher is very angry with the student, but chose to stay cool and talk to the student in private. The teacher did not take the misbehavior personally and acknowledged the student's feelings. The student learned her teacher cares about her.

{SECTION 1: POSITIVE BEHAVIOR BASICS}

Revenge Seeking

 Children often feel disappointed and hurt too!

Ways to positively calm a child:

- ✓ Build a strong relationship with the child
- ✓ Stay calm and cool
- ✓ Acknowledge feelings
- ✓ Listen to the child

Don't!

- ✗ Lose control
- ✗ Display anger
- ✗ Retaliate
- ✗ Punish
- ✗ Get even

Remember

When students display revengeful behavior, don't take it personally!

By staying cool and acknowledging a child's feelings you can help the child calm down.

{SECTION 1: POSITIVE BEHAVIOR BASICS}

Display of Inadequacy

With display of inadequacy, everyone feels like giving up. Have you ever felt discouraged enough to quit? A child who is demonstrating display of inadequacy desperately needs to achieve some success. If adults feel like giving up on a child, how can the child be motivated to continue to try? Consider the following to recognize whether or not a child is seeking display of inadequacy.

How do I feel when the child misbehaves?

Hopeless or discouraged

How do I respond to the misbehavior?

Giving up or completing the task yourself

What is the child's response?

No improvement; gives up

What does the child really need?

The child needs lots of encouragement from you! Show you believe in the child and his/her ability to achieve success. Teachers can break the task into smaller steps to help make it easier for the student to understand. Encourage every positive attempt, and communicate that you are not going to give up on them. Offer support in helping each child reach their personal goal.

Show you believe in the child and his/her ability to achieve success.

Display of Inadequacy – Incorrect Response

When a teacher feels discouraged or hopeless, the student may decide to give up.

(SECTION 1: POSITIVE BEHAVIOR BASICS)

Display of Inadequacy – Correct Response

The teacher does not become discouraged when the student wants to give up. The teacher acknowledges the student's feelings, and continues to offer help. The student learned her teacher believes in her and will never give up.

Display of Inadequacy – Incorrect Response

The teacher is communicating she agrees the student can't learn and has given up by completing the task for him.

{SECTION 1: POSITIVE BEHAVIOR BASICS}

Display of Inadequacy – Correct Response

The teacher does not become discouraged when the student wants to give up. The teacher breaks the task into smaller steps and continues to offer help. The student learned his teacher believes in him and will never give up.

{SECTION 1: POSITIVE BEHAVIOR BASICS}

Display of Inadequacy

 Everyone feels discouraged enough to give up sometimes.

Ways to positively keep students trying:

- ✓ Recognize every positive attempt
- ✓ Break task into smaller steps
- ✓ Acknowledge feelings
- ✓ Listen to the child
- ✓ Offer your help
- ✓ Offer encouragement
- ✓ Give support

Don't!

- ✗ Do the task yourself
- ✗ Give up
- ✗ Agree with child
- ✗ Act hopeless
- ✗ Act helpless

Remember: When students demonstrate display of inadequacy, they are very frustrated with a task. By calmly offering your help and encouraging every positive attempt, there is nothing a student can't learn!

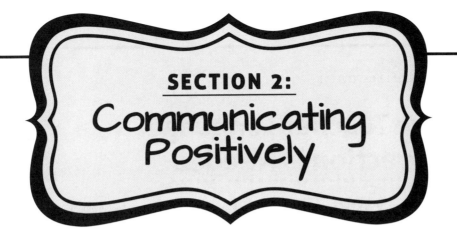

SECTION 2: Communicating Positively

Verbalize the Good!

Compliment and praise everything you observe students do that follows your rules and procedures!

Ignore what you can!

Re-teach the desired behavior when students forget, and compliment those students as soon as they follow your directions!

✳ Talk to students about problem behavior in private only!

{SECTION 2: COMMUNICATING POSITIVELY}

Ineffective Teacher Language When Correction is Needed

 Whether in public or private statements like these increase the likelihood of misbehavior!

"I have told you four times to finish your work!"

"You know how to keep your hands and feet to yourself."

"That is not responsible behavior!"

"I'm trying to get you ready for middle school."

"You need to listen to me!"

"What do you think you are doing?"

"Take a time out!"

"That's five minutes off recess."

"I'm calling for the principal!"

Effective Teacher Language When Correction is Needed

To students in private…

"How can I help you?"

"What do you need?"

"How can you use respect right now?"

"I need your help to be sure everyone is treated with respect."

"I understand but now's the time to _____."

To the class…

"How many of you can hear when more than one person is talking?"

{SECTION 2: COMMUNICATING POSITIVELY}

Ineffective Parent Language When Correction is Needed

 Whether in public or private statements like these increase the likelihood of misbehavior!

"I have told you four times to clean your room!"

"You know what I expect."

"That is not respectful behavior!"

"Do it because I said so."

"You need to listen to me!"

"What do you think you are doing?"

"Wait until your father gets home!"

"I don't have time for this mess."

"You know I'm a single parent!"

"You are grounded until school is out!"

"No television for a month!"

"Why do you always question me?"

Effective Parent Language When Correction is Needed

To child in private...

"How can I help you?"

"What do you need?"

"How can you show me respect right now?"

"I need your help so we can get out the door on time."

"I understand but now is the time to _____."

To child with others present...

"Let's talk one at a time so we can hear each other."

"If you share you will enjoy playing together. Have you thought about taking turns?"

(SECTION 2: COMMUNICATING POSITIVELY)

Positive Discipline Works for Parents

Children need to be given attention and feel a sense of belonging just as adults do. When children don't feel like they belong, and they can't get attention in useful ways, they seek attention through misbehavior.

When children are misbehaving, if we focus on what they are doing well (by telling them specifically what we like) their behavior will improve. This may sound too simplistic, but I've seen it work many times. A child in a classroom is being disruptive day after day. The teacher finds something the child is doing well and tells him, "Johnny, I like how you remembered to raise your hand." Guess what—Johnny liked that praise and will raise his hand more often to get it. Johnny also will probably listen to the teacher more and be more cooperative. As the teacher continues to notice Johnny's good behavior, he will continue to seek that positive attention.

As parents you can use this technique at home. Try focusing more on what your child is doing well. For example, your child often complains about homework and doesn't want to complete it. Be sure to notice when your child completes his homework without a fuss. Say something like, "Johnny, I like how you completed your homework right away. It's written so neatly, too." Guess what—Johnny feels happy he made the choice to complete the homework without a fuss, and he will repeat the behavior.

Our children are no different from us in how they feel. They want to feel valued and successful, just as we do. So, point out what your children are doing well, tell them specifically how they are special, and point out the good choices they make. Remember to focus on the positive! There are no limits to what our children can accomplish!

SECTION 3: A School-wide Plan for Teaching Behavior

School-wide Expectations

As previously explained, behavior must be taught in our schools. With a school full of staff teaching behavior at the beginning of each school year, why have a different set of rules in every classroom? Why not have a consistent set of rules and expectations throughout the school? It just makes sense!

Imagine the power associated with a school-wide rule and set of behavior expectations? Students would be taught the behavioral expectations in kindergarten at the beginning of their school career. With the same set of behavioral expectations taught and reinforced again in first grade, the student will learn and understand what is expected at school even better. We all learn new skills better when they are repeatedly taught over and over again. Think of how well a student would have learned the expected behavior at school by fifth grade if taught the same behavioral expectations every year since kindergarten!

> ❋ Why not have a consistent set of rules and expectations throughout the school?

Students will demonstrate positive behavior more frequently in a school that has decided to teach the same rule throughout the building. A word of caution is needed here however—the staff in the school must use the same language when teaching the rule and associated behavioral expectations. Particularly with young children developing language, if teachers are using different words the students may confuse what the school expects. Likewise, older students who have more than one teacher can become confused as well. It is critical school staff decide exactly what they want the school-wide rule and behavioral expectations to be and everyone agrees to support it!

{SECTION 3: A SCHOOL-WIDE PLAN FOR TEACHING BEHAVIOR}

✱ A catchy acronym for the rule is helpful. A sample school-wide rule is SOAR, with sample lesson plans for teaching the behavioral expectations in all areas of the school.

SOAR Rule

SOAR works beautifully as an acronym for a school-wide rule for many school mascots—hawk, eagle, or any other kind of bird. You could also use **SOAR** to refer to "SOARing Stars" or balloons, a rocketship, etc.

Safety

Organization

Achievement

Respect

{SECTION 3: A SCHOOL-WIDE PLAN FOR TEACHING BEHAVIOR}

{SECTION 3: A SCHOOL-WIDE PLAN FOR TEACHING BEHAVIOR}

SOAR Rule Chart

School Behavioral Standards	Bus	Hallway	Classroom
Safety	Stay in seat. Keep hands, feet, and property to self.	Walk on the right with hands by your side.	Keep hands, feet, and objects to yourself.
Organization	Book bag in lap.	Watch where you walk.	Listen and follow directions.
Achievement	Show good citizenship.	Walk directly to your destination.	Raise your hand to speak.
Respect	Speak kindly and quietly.	Speak kindly and quietly.	Be kind to others.

 The idea for a Teaching Matrix came from George Sugai & Robert Horner's "School-wide Positive Behavior Support: Basics" Power Point, Center on Positive Behavioral Interventions and Supports, University of Oregon, June 8, 2005.

Media Center & Computer Lab	**Cafeteria**	**Playground**	**Restroom**
Walk	Walk in line.	Maintain personal space.	Maintain personal space. Wash hands.
Have library card ready. Return books on time.	Stay in line.	Bring in equipment. Line up at teacher signal.	Be as quick as possible.
Read on your level.	Stay seated at your table.	Have a plan.	Develop personal hygiene.
Whisper Share equipment. Treat materials carefully.	Throw away trash and return tray. Speak kindly and quietly after you finish eating.	Use equipment properly. Pick up litter. Include others in your games.	Be neat and clean.

{SECTION 3: A SCHOOL-WIDE PLAN FOR TEACHING BEHAVIOR}

Reproducible Classroom Posters

Grades: 1-5

The SOAR Rule should be displayed in all classrooms so it can be continually referred to by the teachers.

Achievement

Raise your hand to speak.

Organization

Listen and follow directions.

Achievement

Raise your hand to speak.

School-wide Lesson Plans

This plan will be much more effective if all staff use the same language.

The following lesson plans should be taught and reinforced in all homeroom classes.

(SECTION 3: A SCHOOL-WIDE PLAN FOR TEACHING BEHAVIOR)

Bus Behavioral Standards	**Instruction** *Students brainstorm*	**Instruction** *Teacher Talk*	**Acknowledgement** *Positive Talk*
Safety	*Examples:* Stay in seat. Keep hands, feet, and property to self.	"Safety on the bus means we stay in our seat. We keep our hands, feet, and property to self." *(Teacher demonstrates sitting on a bus seat with hands folded in lap. Have students practice.)*	"That is how we stay safe on the bus. Thanks for practicing with me." "Thanks for showing me you know how to be safe on the bus."
Organization	*Examples:* Book bag in lap.	"Organization on the bus means we keep our book bags in our laps." *(Teacher demonstrates sitting on a bus seat with a book bag in lap. Have students practice.)*	"That is how we stay organized on the bus. Thanks for practicing with me." "Thanks for showing me you know how to be organized on the bus."
Achievement	*Examples:* Show good citizenship; follow the rules and encourage others to.	"Achievement on the bus means we show good citizenship by following all the rules." *(Teacher demonstrates sitting on a bus seat with a book bag in lap and reminding another student to do this. Have students practice.)*	"That is how we show achievement on the bus. Thanks for practicing with me." "Thanks for showing me you know how to achieve on the bus."
Respect	*Examples:* Speak kindly and quietly. Use words like hello, please, thank you.	"Respect on the bus means we speak kindly and quietly." *(Teacher demonstrates saying hello to a friend and asking if they had a good day. Have students practice.)*	"That is how we show respect on the bus. Thanks for practicing with me." "Thanks for showing me you can be respectful on the bus."

{SECTION 3: A SCHOOL-WIDE PLAN FOR TEACHING BEHAVIOR}

Hallway Behavioral Standards	Instruction *Students brainstorm*	Instruction *Teacher Talk*	Acknowledgement *Positive Talk*
Safety	*Examples:* Walk on the right. Keep hands by side. Stay in line.	"Safety in the hallway means we walk on the right with our hands by our sides." *(Teacher demonstrates walking on the right with hands by side, and then has students practice.)*	"That is how we stay safe in the hallway. Thanks for practicing with me." "Thanks for showing me you know how to stay safe in the hallway."
Organization	*Examples:* Watch where you walk. Stay behind others.	"Organization in the hallway means we watch where we walk." *(Teacher demonstrates how to walk in line while watching those in front. Have students practice.)*	"That is how we stay organized in the hallway. Thanks for practicing with me." "Thanks for showing me you know how to stay organized in the hallway."
Achievement	*Examples:* Walk directly to destination.	"Achievement in the hallway means we walk directly to our destination." *(Teacher demonstrates how to return a book to the media center and then return to class quickly. Have students practice.)*	"That is how we show achievement in the hallway. Thanks for practicing with me." "Thanks for showing me you know how to achieve in the hallway."
Respect	*Examples:* Speak kindly and quietly. Use words like hello, please, thank you.	"Respect in the hallway means we speak kindly and quietly." *(Teacher demonstrates saying hello to a friend and asking if they had a good day. Have students practice.)*	"That is how we show respect in the hallway. Thanks for practicing with me." "Thanks for showing me you can be respectful in the hallway."

{SECTION 3: A SCHOOL-WIDE PLAN FOR TEACHING BEHAVIOR}

Classroom Behavioral Standards	Instruction *Students brainstorm*	Instruction *Teacher Talk*	Acknowledgement *Positive Talk*
Safety	*Examples:* Stay in personal space at desk. Stay in personal space on floor. Keep your property to yourself.	"Safety in the classroom means we keep hands, feet, and objects to self." *(Teacher demonstrates sitting in a desk keeping hands, feet, and objects in personal space. Have students practice.)*	"That is how we stay safe in the classroom. Thanks for practicing with me." "Thanks for showing me you know how to stay safe in the classroom."
Organization	*Examples:* Listen by keeping your eyes on the teacher and your body still. Follow teacher directions promptly.	"Organization in the classroom means we listen and follow directions." *(Teacher demonstrates how to follow several directions promptly. Have students practice as teacher gives directions.)*	"That is how we stay organized in the classroom. Thanks for practicing with me." "Thanks for showing me you know how to stay organized in the classroom."
Achievement	*Examples:* Raise your hand and wait to be called on.	"Achievement in the classroom means we raise our hands to speak." *(Teacher demonstrates how to return a book to the media center and then return to class quickly. Have students practice.)*	"That is how we show achievement in the classroom. Thanks for practicing with me." "Thanks for showing me you know how to achieve in the classroom."
Respect	*Examples:* Speak kindly and quietly. Use words like hello, please, thank you.	"Respect in the classroom means we speak kindly and quietly." *(Teacher demonstrates saying hello to a friend and asking if they had a good day. Have students practice.)*	"That is how we show respect in the classroom. Thanks for practicing with me." "Thanks for showing me you can be respectful in the classroom."

{SECTION 3: A SCHOOL-WIDE PLAN FOR TEACHING BEHAVIOR}

Media Center/ Computer Lab	**Instruction** *Students brainstorm*	**Instruction** *Teacher Talk*	**Acknowledgement** *Positive Talk*
Safety	*Examples:* Walk. Stay in personal space Follow safety rules for internet use.	"Safety in the media center or computer lab means we walk." *(Teacher demonstrates walking while staying in personal space. Have students practice.)*	"That is how we stay safe in the media center and computer lab. Thanks for practicing with me." "Thanks for showing me you know how to stay safe in the media center and computer lab."
Organization	*Examples:* Walk to circulation desk with books ready for check-out. Return books on time.	"Organization in the media center means we have our library cards ready and return books on time. *(Teacher demonstrates how to walk to circulation desk with library card ready. Have students practice.)*	"That is how we stay organized in the media center. Thanks for practicing with me." "Thanks for showing me you know how to stay organized in the media center."
Achievement	*Examples:* Read on your level.	"Achievement in the media center means we read on our level." *(Teacher demonstrates how to find books on different reading levels. Have students practice.)*	"That is how we show achievement in the media center. Thanks for practicing with me." "Thanks for showing me you know how to achieve in the media center."
Respect	*Examples:* Speak in a whisper. Share equipment. Treat materials carefully.	"Respect in the media center or computer lab means we speak in a whisper, share, and treat materials carefully." *(Teacher demonstrates a whisper and how to share equipment.*	"That is how we show respect in the media center or computer lab. Thanks for practicing with me." "Thanks for showing me you can be respectful in the media center or computer lab."

{SECTION 3: A SCHOOL-WIDE PLAN FOR TEACHING BEHAVIOR}

Cafeteria Standards	Instruction *Students brainstorm*	Instruction *Teacher Talk*	Acknowledgement *Positive Talk*
Safety	*Examples:* Walk. Stay in personal space.	"Safety in the cafeteria means we walk in line." *(Teacher demonstrates walking in line while staying in personal space. Have students practice.)*	"That is how we stay safe in the cafeteria. Thanks for practicing with me." "Thanks for showing me you know how to stay safe in the cafeteria."
Organization	*Examples:* Stay in the cafeteria line. Stay seated while eating.	"Organization in the cafeteria means we stay in our line and stay seated while eating." *(Teacher demonstrates how to walk through the cafeteria line and sit down. Have students practice.)*	"That is how we stay organized in the cafeteria. Thanks for practicing with me." "Thanks for showing me you know how to stay organized in the cafeteria."
Achievement	*Examples:* Choose healthy foods.	"Achievement in the cafeteria means we focus on nutrition." *(Teacher demonstrates how to choose healthy foods in the cafeteria line. Have students practice.)*	"That is how we show achievement in the cafeteria. Thanks for practicing with me." "Thanks for showing me you know how to achieve in the cafeteria."
Respect	*Examples:* Return tray. Throw away trash. Speak quietly when finished eating.	"Respect in the cafeteria means we return our tray and throw away trash. We also speak kindly and quietly when finished eating. *(Teacher demonstrates & students practice.)*	"That is how we show respect in the cafeteria. Thanks for practicing with me." "Thanks for showing me you can be respectful in the cafeteria."

{SECTION 3: A SCHOOL-WIDE PLAN FOR TEACHING BEHAVIOR}

Playground Behavioral Standards	**Instruction** *Students brainstorm*	**Instruction** *Teacher Talk*	**Acknowledgement** *Positive Talk*
Safety	*Examples:* Walk or run. Stay in personal space.	"Safety on the playground means we maintain personal space." *(Outside teacher demonstrates walking & running near others while staying in personal space. Have students practice.)*	"That is how we stay safe on the playground. Thanks for practicing with me." "Thanks for showing me you know how to stay safe on the playground."
Organization	*Examples:* At signal pick up equipment. At signal line up.	"Organization on the playground means we bring in equipment on teacher signal." *(Outside teacher demonstrates how to pick up equipment and line up on teacher signal. Have students practice.)*	"That is how we stay organized on the playground. Thanks for practicing with me." "Thanks for showing me you know how to stay organized on the playground."
Achievement	*Examples:* Choose what you are going to play ahead of time.	"Achievement on the playground means we have a plan." *(Teacher demonstrates how to find books on different reading levels. Have students practice.)*	"That is how we show achievement on the playground. Thanks for practicing with me." "Thanks for showing me you know how to achieve on the playground."
Respect	*Examples:* Use equipment properly. Pick up litter. Include others in play.	"Respect on the playground means we use equipment properly, pick up litter, and include others." *(Outside teacher demonstrates how to use the equipment, where to put litter, and how to ask others to join in games.)*	"That is how we show respect on the playground. Thanks for practicing with me." "Thanks for showing me you can be respectful on the playground."

(SECTION 3: A SCHOOL-WIDE PLAN FOR TEACHING BEHAVIOR)

Restroom Behavioral Standards	**Instruction** *Students brainstorm*	**Instruction** *Teacher Talk*	**Acknowledgement** *Positive Talk*
Safety	*Examples:* Stay in personal space. Wash hands.	"Safety in the restroom means we maintain personal space." *(Teacher discusses how students should keep hands to self while in the restroom. Teacher discusses hand washing and the importance of cleanliness.)*	"That is how we stay safe in the restroom. Thanks for discussing this with me." "Thanks for telling me you know how to stay safe in the restroom."
Organization	*Examples:* Exit the restroom as soon as you are finished.	"Organization in the restroom means we are as quick as possible." *(Teacher discusses how students should enter and exit the restroom quickly.)*	"That is how we stay organized in the restroom. Thanks for discussing this with me." "Thanks for telling me you know how to stay organized in the restroom."
Achievement	*Examples:* Wash hands. Throw away paper towels.	"Achievement in the restroom means we develop personal hygiene." *(Teacher discusses cleanliness in the bathroom—washing hands and throwing away paper towels.)*	"That is how we show cleanliness in the restroom. Thanks for discussing this with me."
Respect	*Examples:* Use restroom with care. Keep restroom as clean as possible.	"Respect in the restroom means be neat and clean." *(Teacher asks students to give examples of being neat and clean in the restroom.)*	"That is how we show respect in the restroom. Thanks for discussing this with me." "Thanks for telling me how you can be respectful in the restroom."

SOARing with Teacher Encouragement

✳ **Praise in public...**

"Thank you for remembering to keep your hands by your side in the hallway! You are showing **SAFETY**."

"Everyone is listening and following directions well! That keeps us all **ORGANIZED**."

"You all raised your hands and participated so well during math today. Good job with **ACHIEVEMENT!**"

"Thanks for showing **RESPECT** while we had a visitor in our classroom!"

"Because everyone followed the **SOAR Rule** so well today, we have time for an extra five minutes of recess!

{SECTION 3: A SCHOOL-WIDE PLAN FOR TEACHING BEHAVIOR}

School-wide Rewards

Most students will choose positive behavior when they are taught the school-wide expectations and then receive rewards for exhibiting that appropriate behavior. Therefore, just as a school-wide system of rules is necessary, so is a school-wide system for rewarding positive behavior.

❋ **Some suggestions for school-wide rewards:**

✓ SOAR Coins—given to students for positive behavior. Students collect the coins and purchase items with them. All staff, even bus drivers and cafeteria staff, can reward students with SOAR coins. (Coins in various colors for good behavior are available at Oriental Trading and Walmart.)

✓ SOAR Store—contains a variety of different items for purchase with SOAR coins. Start with school supplies at the beginning of the year, and add craft supplies, books, and toys later. Many businesses will donate items if you share the school's positive behavioral system.

✓ SOAR post cards—mailed to parents with "Good News" about behavior.

✓ SOAR slips—given to students listing positive behavior exhibited. A copy can be added to a SOAR box in the front office for a special drawing on Fridays. SOAR slips ready for duplication are found on the following two pages.

✓ SOAR stamps—create a stamp with SOAR and a hawk, rocket, or balloon on it. Stamp papers to reward good student work.

{SECTION 3: A SCHOOL-WIDE PLAN FOR TEACHING BEHAVIOR}

SOAR Slip Rewards

Student name _____

Grade: _____

Date _____

S: Safety _____

O: Organization _____

A: Achievement _____

R: Respect _____

Teacher signature:
_____

Student name _____

Grade: _____

Date _____

S: Safety _____

O: Organization _____

A: Achievement _____

R: Respect _____

Teacher signature:
_____

Student name _____

Grade: _____

Date _____

S: Safety _____

O: Organization _____

A: Achievement _____

R: Respect _____

Teacher signature:
_____

Student name _____

Grade: _____

Date _____

S: Safety _____

O: Organization _____

A: Achievement _____

R: Respect _____

Teacher signature:
_____

{SECTION 3: A SCHOOL-WIDE PLAN FOR TEACHING BEHAVIOR}

SOAR Slip Rewards

# SOARing Student

Student name _____

Grade: _____

Date _____

S: Safety _____

O: Organization _____

A: Achievement _____

R: Respect _____

Teacher signature:
_____

SOARing Student

Student name _____

Grade: _____

Date _____

S: Safety _____

O: Organization _____

A: Achievement _____

R: Respect _____

Teacher signature:
_____

# SOARing Student

Student name _____

Grade: _____

Date _____

S: Safety _____

O: Organization _____

A: Achievement _____

R: Respect _____

Teacher signature:
_____

# SOARing Student

Student name _____

Grade: _____

Date _____

S: Safety _____

O: Organization _____

A: Achievement _____

R: Respect _____

Teacher signature:
_____

{SECTION 3: A SCHOOL-WIDE PLAN FOR TEACHING BEHAVIOR}

SOAR Slip Rewards

Student name _____

Grade: _____

Date _____

S: Safety _____

O: Organization _____

A: Achievement _____

R: Respect _____

Teacher signature:

_____

Student name _____

Grade: _____

Date _____

S: Safety _____

O: Organization _____

A: Achievement _____

R: Respect _____

Teacher signature:

_____

Student name _____

Grade: _____

Date _____

S: Safety _____

O: Organization _____

A: Achievement _____

R: Respect _____

Teacher signature:

_____

SOARing Student

Student name _____

Grade: _____

Date _____

S: Safety _____

O: Organization _____

A: Achievement _____

R: Respect _____

Teacher signature:

_____

{SECTION 3: A SCHOOL-WIDE PLAN FOR TEACHING BEHAVIOR}

SOAR Cheer!

Hey everybody, have you heard the talk?

Yep, that's right! I'm a Windsor Hill Hawk!

I'm here to be the best that I can,

learning and sharing with my fellow man.

Now stand back folks and watch me fly.

This ol' Hawk's gonna touch the sky!

The wind's beneath my wings for sure.

Look at me! I'm ready to SOAR!

S-O-A-R! - SOAR!

The SOAR Cheer was written by Cariene Keadle,
3rd grade teacher at Windsor Hill Arts Infused Elementary School.
It is reprinted here with her permission.

SECTION 4:
Classroom Activities & Lessons

Morning Meetings

A great way to set positive communication as the expectation for the day is by conducting a Morning Meeting! Make a ten to fifteen minute meeting with your class a part of your daily routine! Simply begin by circling students in a group on the carpet. Have students greet each other and share. There are many books already written on Class or Morning Meetings that are full of awesome ideas. On the next page are listed a few of my favorites that I have seen in action!

※ Have students greet each other and share.

{SECTION 4: CLASSROOM ACTIVITIES & LESSONS}

Positive Ways to Greet

- ✓ Each student has a turn to state his/her name with an action. Ex: Rachel claps twice as she says her name. John makes a salute as he states his name. Students state all the names with actions, before adding their own.

- ✓ A student says "hello" to the student next to him/her and then gives the student a compliment. Go around the circle until everyone has had a turn.

- ✓ A student tosses a nerf ball to another student. The student who catches the ball, says something kind to the student who tossed the ball. Take turns around the circle until everyone has had a turn.

Sharing Feelings

- ✓ Each student is given a turn to show a "thumbs up" or "thumbs down" and explain.

- ✓ A student "makes a face" to show how he/she is feeling. The other students guess the feeling, and then the student shares why he/she is feeling that way. Let every student have a turn.

Don't make a student participate in the Morning Meeting. As the student watches the fun, he/she will eventually join in.

Celebrate Success

✱ One of the best ways to promote positive behavior in the classroom is to periodically involve students in fun, community building activities. Students will learn to look for the good in everyone, and will be encouraged to make good choices themselves.

Pat on the Back: Students trace around a hand on cardstock and cut it out. Students write the name of a friend, along with a compliment to that friend, and then give it to him or her.

Drum Roll: When a student has achieved something good, give him/her a drum roll and make an announcement of congratulations to the class.

Standing Ovation: Same as the drum roll, except the class gives a standing ovation to a student that achieved something good.

Good News Journals: All students decorate a "Good News" Journal. At the end of each school day everyone is asked to write a daily accomplishment or positive event that occurred.

Tada!! Look yourself in the mirror, smile at yourself, and give yourself a "Tada!" for something or for nothing at all!

(SECTION 4: CLASSROOM ACTIVITIES & LESSONS

Let's SOAR Together

Grades: 1-5

Objective: To teach students how they can help each other to make good decisions.

Materials:

- A puzzle piece duplicated on cardstock for each student (cut the pieces out along the dotted lines only)
- Pencils
- Crayons or colored pencils
- Poster board in your favorite color
- Glue

Directions:

1. Give each student as well as yourself a puzzle piece. (If students are sitting in groups, it might work best to give each group the pieces to the same letter.)

2. Print your name in the center of your piece and ask students to do the same.

3. Show students the pictures representing different subjects from the following page and ask students to draw their favorite on the puzzle piece. Demonstrate by drawing your favorite on your piece.

4. Students may then color their puzzle piece however they wish. Make sure you color yours too! It works best if you use crayons or colored pencils instead of markers.

5. After everyone has finished, put the pieces together on top of a piece of poster board. Students will be excited to see that the puzzle spells SOAR! Explain everyone in class is expected to follow the SOAR rule! Every member of the class needs to SOAR so we can all learn and do our best!

(SECTION 4: CLASSROOM ACTIVITIES & LESSONS)

Let's SOAR Together (continued)

GRADES: 1-5

Discussion Questions:

1. What happens if one member of the class forgets to show—
   - Safety?
   - Organization?
   - Achievement?
   - Respect?

2. How can we help one another to show—
   - Safety?
   - Organization?
   - Achievement?
   - Respect?

3. What is our class like when everyone follows the SOAR rule?

(SECTION 4: CLASSROOM ACTIVITIES & LESSONS

Let's SOAR Together—Favorite Subjects

reading

science

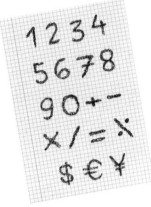

math

music

social studies

art

p.e.

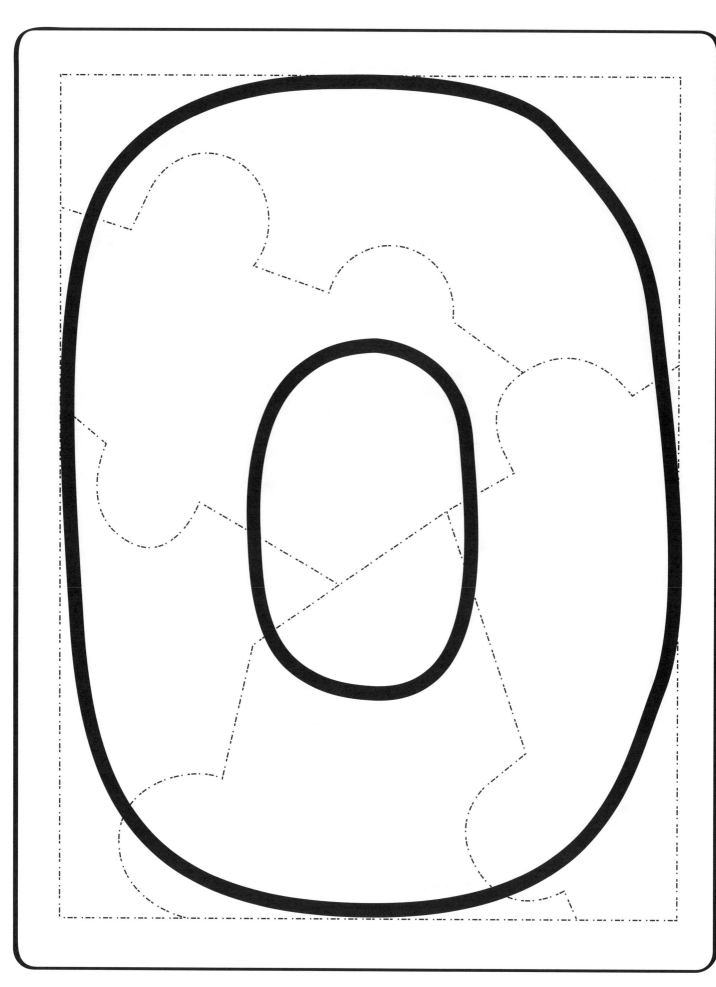

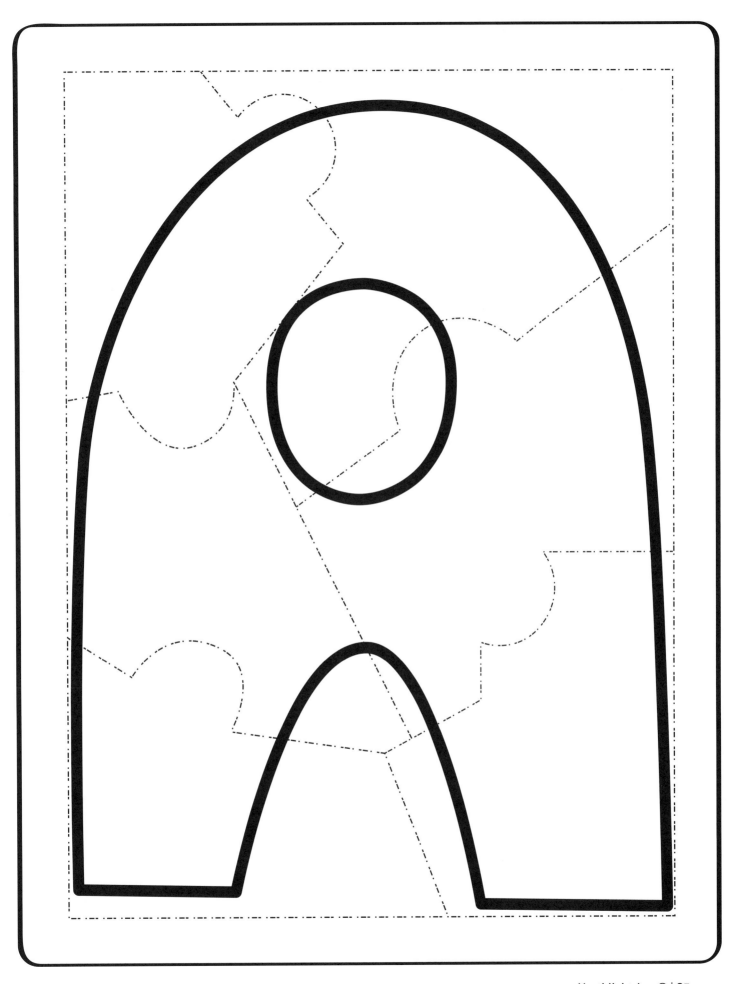

{SECTION 4: CLASSROOM ACTIVITIES AND LESSONS}

You Deserve a Trophy

GRADES: 1-5

 Objective: To help students feel proud of their accomplishments at school, so they will desire to continue doing their best.

Materials:
- Trophy cutout printed on cardstock and cut out for each student

Directions:

1. Ask students to define "accomplishment." Discuss that an accomplishment is something that is done successfully. It could be a specific skill or an improvement in behavior.

2. As students brainstorm different accomplishments of theirs and others list them on the board. Make sure students include social skills as well as measureable achievements.

3. Give students a copy of the trophy that follows. Have students write their name on the plaque of the trophy. Next, students should write or draw a picture of their accomplishment that they are most proud of on the trophy.

4. Encourage the children to share one of their accomplishments aloud with the class. Discuss how they feel about their accomplishments.

5. Suggest that the children take their trophy home and tape it to their mirror. Ask them to look into the mirror each morning after getting dressed and read their accomplishment aloud. Remind the students that with effort they can reach their goals!

{SECTION 4: CLASSROOM ACTIVITIES AND LESSONS}

{SECTION 4: CLASSROOM ACTIVITIES AND LESSONS}

Let's Juggle Together

GRADES: K-5

 Overview: Juggling is a wonderful activity to help build community in a classroom. Every child can learn to juggle with enough practice and help.

Objective: As students learn to juggle they will realize that mistakes are okay. Juggling also helps students realize that with practice and persistence they can be successful in reaching any (behavioral or academic) goal.

Materials:
- 3 scarves (must be different colors) for each student
- Juggling diagram

Directions:

1. Teach the students how to juggle one scarf, then two. (Third through fifth grade students may learn how to juggle three scarves.) The "Juggling Directions" page that follows is helpful to enlarge and scan so that students have a visual of what they will be attempting to do.

2. Start with one scarf. Toss it up with one hand and catch it with the other hand. Repeat back and forth until comfortable.

3. With two scarves, one in each hand, toss up the right one and then follow with the left one in a crisscross motion. Catch the first scarf with your left hand and the second one with your right hand as they float down. Say to yourself, "1, 2, catch, catch." Repeat until comfortable. You can stop here if you choose and pat yourself on the back. If you want to try three scarves, continue.

Youthlight, Inc. © | 87

(SECTION 4: CLASSROOM ACTIVITIES AND LESSONS)

With three scarves, you'll need to hold two scarves in the right hand (one between thumb and forefinger, the other between forefinger and middle finger) and one in the left hand. Using the same crisscross motion, release one of the two scarves first, then the left-handed scarf then back to the remaining scarf in the right hand. You will catch the first scarf with the left hand as soon as the left scarf is released, then continue saying to yourself, "1, 2, 3, 1, 2, 3" as you toss the scarves in the air. Expect to drop scarves and have to start over many times. Keep practicing 5-10 minutes every day until you can keep all three scarves moving through the air.

Discussion Questions:

1. How many of you had fun learning to juggle?
2. What other feelings did you have? Did you feel frustrated?
3. How did you keep your behavior under control when you felt frustrated?
4. How did we show "safety" while learning to juggle?
5. Did we have to demonstrate "organization" abilities?
6. How did we show "achievement?"
7. Was "respect" important as you learned to juggle? Why?

Juggling Directions

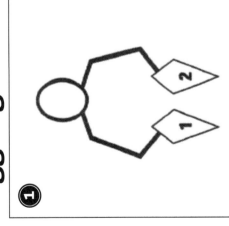

1. Begin with a scarf in each hand.

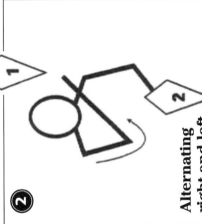

2. Alternating right and left in a criss-cross motion, toss scarf 1 across your body and into the air.

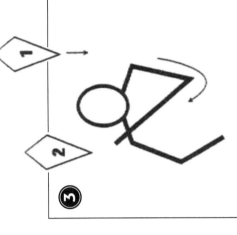

3. Then toss scarf 2 across your body into the air. For a moment, both scarves are in the air.

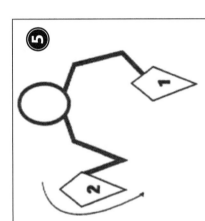

4. To catch, reach straight up in front of you with left hand and catch scarf 1 coming down.

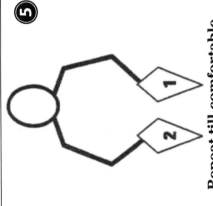

5. Then catch scarf 2 likewise with right hand.

5. Repeat till comfortable saying to yourself: "One, two, catch, catch."

To juggle 3 scarves, use the same criss-cross motion. Begin with scarves 1 & 2 in your right hand and scarf 3 in your left. Alternate tossing right, left, right, catch, catch, catch.

(SECTION 4: CLASSROOM ACTIVITIES AND LESSONS)

Let's Keep Rolling!

Grades: 1-5

 Objective: To teach students positive behavior and remind them of what to do to make good decisions.

Materials:

- List of questions numbered #1-#12 on the following page. You can scan them into a Power Point or Smart board, or list them on the board.
- One set of dice

Directions:

1. Explain to the class that you are all going to play a game to help everyone remember the SOAR rule!
2. Divide the class into two teams.
3. Each student will have a turn to walk to the front of the room, roll the dice on a table, and then answer the corresponding question. For example, if a student rolls the number 10, then that student answers question number 10.
4. If the student can correctly answer the question without help then the team gets 10 points. If the student answers incorrectly, the team gets no points.
5. If the student needs help, then he/she may ask another student for the answer. If that student answers correctly the team earns 5 points. If that student answers incorrectly, the team gets no points.
6. Once a student answers the question incorrectly it is always the next teams turn to answer that question and then roll the dice.
7. Once every student has had a turn to play the game is over and points are totaled.

{SECTION 4: CLASSROOM ACTIVITIES AND LESSONS}

✳ Let's Keep Rolling! Questions

1. What is our school-wide rule?
2. How do you show "safety" in the classroom?
3. How do you show "organization" in the classroom?
4. How do you show "achievement" in the classroom?
5. How do you show "respect" in the classroom?
6. Name one way to SOAR on the bus.
7. Name one way to SOAR in the cafeteria.
8. If you participate in lessons by raising your hand to speak, what part of SOAR are you demonstrating?
9. If you whisper in the media center, what part of SOAR are you demonstrating?
10. Name one way to show respect in our building.
11. Name one way to help another student achieve.
12. Name one way to help yourself achieve.

{SECTION 4: CLASSROOM ACTIVITIES AND LESSONS}

SOAR & More!

GRADES: K-5

 Objective: To teach students a school-wide rule and remind them of the expected behaviors.

Materials:

- S, O, A, and R cards duplicated on cardstock and cut apart
- Pencils, crayons, and colored pencils

Directions:

1. Distribute the S, O, A, and R cards so that every student has a complete set.

2. Hold up the "S" card and ask students to name what part of our rule the "S" stands for? (Safety) Write "Safety" on the board and tell students to complete the word on their card by adding the "afety" after the capital S. Repeat with each card for every letter in S-O-A-R. (Organization, Achievement, Respect)

3. Have students brainstorm ways to show "Safety" at school—keep hands on top of desk, keep feet under desk, stay in your personal space when in the class line, etc. Ask students to draw their favorite way to show safety on their safety card. Repeat this process for "Organization, Achievement, and Respect."

4. Allow students time to color their cards (this would be a good activity to finish after completing other assignments).

5. This activity would work to teach any school-wide rule! Ex: 3 R's—Respectful, Responsible, and Ready to learn or 3 Be's—Be safe, Be kind, Be responsible.

{SECTION 4: CLASSROOM ACTIVITIES AND LESSONS}

SOAR & More! Cards

S	O
A	R

Youthlight, Inc. © | 93

{SECTION 4: CLASSROOM ACTIVITIES AND LESSONS}

To Tell or Not to Tell

GRADES: K-5

 Objectives: To teach students that when someone is in danger or needs help it is important to tell an adult. Students will also learn that "tattling" is inappropriate.

Materials:

- *A Bad Case of Tattle Tongue* by Julia Cook, available through YouthLight, Inc.
- Two popsicle sticks for each student with a red "Stop" sign (don't tell) on one stick and a green "Go"(tell) sign on the other stick.

Directions:

1. Explain that many times students tell the teacher things that are not important and are considered "tattling." The objective of today's lesson is to learn about when you should tell the teacher something and when you should not.

2. Read *A Bad Case of Tattle Tongue,* to the students.

3. Discuss the "Tattle Rules." Make sure the students understand the importance of telling an adult only when they know someone is in trouble or danger.

4. As you read each of the following problems have students decide whether to hold up the red "Stop" sign for not tattling or the green "Go" sign for telling.

   - You see two friends arguing. (red-don't tell)
   - You saw Jimmy pull the fire alarm. (green-tell)
   - Sarah didn't do her homework. (red-don't tell)
   - Sam refuses to play basketball with you. (red-don't tell)
   - Two students are fighting at recess. (green-tell)

To Tell or Not to Tell . . . continued

5. Let students take turns stating a problem with everyone responding using their signs.

6. Duplicate these signs by copying them on card stock using a color printer or cutting them out of construction paper. Then tape or glue each sign to a popsicle stick.

{SECTION 4: CLASSROOM ACTIVITIES AND LESSONS}

I'm In a Pickle

Grades: 1-5

Objectives: To teach students that thinking positively can help them make good behavior choices. Students will practice thinking positive thoughts, and verbalizing them, when faced with a problem.

Materials:
- "Pickle" cards duplicated on cardstock and cut out.

Directions:

1. Explain to the students that everyone has problems. When a problem occurs we can think negatively (which usually makes the problem worse) or we can think positively (which usually helps).

2. For example, you might think you hear classmates talking about you. You can decide they are talking ugly and get upset (negative thinking) or you can decide that perhaps they are saying something good about you (positive thinking) and ignore it.

3. Have students take turns choosing a pickle, then reading it to the class, and deciding how to handle the problem in a positive way.

4. Pass out copies of blank "pickles" and let students write their own problems for the class to discuss anonymously.

{SECTION 4: CLASSROOM ACTIVITIES AND LESSONS}

I'm In a Pickle, continued

✱ Questions:

1. What happens when you think negatively about a problem?

2. What happens when you think positively about a problem?

You studied a long time for your Science test last night, but still failed it today.

You lied to your parents so you are on restriction for a week.

You don't understand your Math homework and are afraid to ask for help.

{SECTION 4: CLASSROOM ACTIVITIES AND LESSONS}

I'm In a Pickle, continued

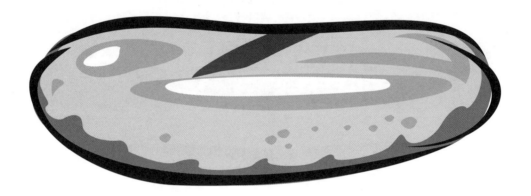

Your parents keep arguing and yelling at each other.

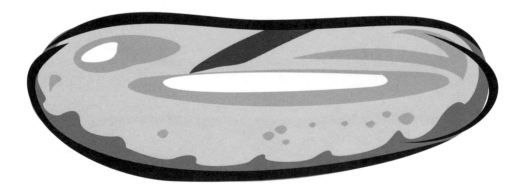

{SECTION 4: CLASSROOM ACTIVITIES AND LESSONS}

Respect is the Key

GRADES: K-5

 Objective: To teach students what it means to show respect for others.

Materials:

- Board or chart tablet for writing
- "Key" worksheet duplicated for each student
- Pencils, crayons or colored pencils

Directions:

1. Write the word respect on the chart tablet.

2. Have students brainstorm respectful words and actions. As students name the words write them on the chart tablet. Ex: please, thank you, kindness, share, helpful, good manners, take turns, caring, etc. (If the students are in kindergarten or first grade, it is helpful to draw a picture next to each word.)

3. Distribute the "key" worksheets. Explain to the students that they will write or draw pictures on their "key" that represent respect. The list on the chart tablet should help them.

4. After most of the students are finished, have them share their "key" one at a time with the other students.

Questions:

1. What are your favorite ways to show respect?

2. How do you feel when students treat you with respect?

3. Should you treat others with respect? Why?

{SECTION 4: CLASSROOM ACTIVITIES AND LESSONS}

Respect is the Key

Name _____

{SECTION 4: CLASSROOM ACTIVITIES AND LESSONS}

Don't Break the Chain

Grades: K-5

 Objective: To reinforce the belief that everyone is happy and learns more when students are demonstrating positive behavior.

Materials:
- Three pieces of paper for sentence strips to give to each student (bright colors work best)
- Pencils

Directions:

1. Ask the students to think about what makes them happy in the classroom. As students share, hopefully someone will explain they are happy when everyone is behaving well.

2. Have students name the classroom rules and then describe the correct behaviors to demonstrate in class.

3. List the appropriate behaviors on the board. Ex. Sit with your feet under your desk. Keep your hands to yourself. Listen when someone else is talking. Complete your written work. Raise your hand to speak. Be kind to others.

4. Give each student two or three sentence strips, depending on the size of your class.

6. Tell the students to write a positive behavior on each sentence strip.

7. Staple the ends of each student's sentence strip together; link the strips as you go.

Don't Break the Chain, continued

8. Have students take turns coming to the front of the room and telling their classmates the good behaviors they are going to show in class.

9. As each student comes, staple his/her connected strips to the others. Staple or tape the chain across the front of the classroom; you want it to stretch from one side of the room to the other.

✽ Questions:

1. What happens when a student breaks one of the classroom rules? How does it make you feel?

2. What would happen to this chain if one link broke?

3. How can we make sure everyone is happy and learning in class?

4. What behavior choices will you make today?

{SECTION 4: CLASSROOM ACTIVITIES AND LESSONS}

Yes, I Can

GRADES: 2-5

 Objective: To review what students need to remember to be successful in the classroom.

Materials:

- "Yes, I Can" worksheets duplicated for students
- Pencils

Directions:

1. Explain to the students that they are going to review how to be successful in class, by completing a fun worksheet.

2. Distribute worksheets to the students.

3. Call on a student to read the first sentence.

4. Explain the scrambled letters make a word that completes the sentence.

5. Tell them the answer to the first sentence—rules.

6. Have another student reread the first sentence.

7. The students will complete the rest of the worksheet by themselves.

8. When everyone is finished, have students take turns sharing their answers by reading a completed sentence.

9. Divide students into groups of three or four. Each group is to choose one of the sentences to act out. As each group role plays, the other students guess which sentence/rule they are acting out.

{SECTION 4: CLASSROOM ACTIVITIES AND LESSONS}

Yes, I Can

Name _____

Directions: Unscramble the words to complete each sentence.

1. I will choose to follow the school _____ (lrUse).

2. I can keep my hands to _____ (flymse).

3. I can keep my feet under my _____ (sekd).

4. When a teacher is talking, I will _____ (ensilt).

5. When lining up, I will stay in my personal _____ (psaec).

6. I can complete all my class work and _____ (rowkomhe).

7. I will participate in class and answer _____ (onuqestis).

8. I will make sure I walk in the school _____ (ldginbui).

9. I can show respect by being helpful and _____ (dkin).

10. I will have lots of _____ (ndfeirs).

(SECTION 5: SMALL GROUP ACTIVITIES AND LESSONS)

You are Lucky!

Grades: K-5

 Objective: To help students begin to know each other and feel a part of the group.

Materials:
- Lucky Charms' cereal
- Napkins
- Plastic Disposable gloves

Directions:

1. Tell the students that they are lucky to be chosen as part of this group which will help them be even more successful in class.

2. Have each student give a simple introduction by sharing their name and classroom teacher.

3. Explain that we are going to play a Lucky Charms' game to get to know each other better.

4. Hand out napkins and with a plastic disposable glove, place a handful of Lucky Charms' cereal on each napkin. Be sure to give yourself some cereal too!

5. Ask students to group the cereal by color—pink, yellow, green, blue, purple. Tell them they may eat the multi-colored marshmallows and the O's.

6. Model answering a question according to the number of each color you have. For example, the question for pink is "What are your favorite sports?" Name a favorite sport for each pink you have; then have students take turns doing the same. Repeat for each color.

    Yellow – What are your favorite animals?
    Green – What are your favorite foods?
    Blue – What are your favorite subjects?
    Green – What do you want us to know about you?

{SECTION 5: SMALL GROUP ACTIVITIES AND LESSONS}

Safety Always!

Grades: K-5

 Objective: To teach students how to keep their hands, feet, and objects to self in all situations.

Materials:
- Art supplies—crayons, markers, scissors, glue
- Sheets of bulletin board paper—one long strip & one large rectangle

Directions:

1. Ask students what safety in the classroom means. Safety in the classroom means you keep your hands, feet, and objects to self. For everyone to be safe, you must stay in your personal space. Explain to the students that they are going to practice staying in their personal space in several different situations.

2. Students discuss and practice personal space in these situations:
   Sitting in their seat • Sharing materials at a table
   Lining up • Sitting on the floor

3. Explain that sometimes in school students are asked to sit or stand even closer. Practice having students sit on the bulletin board paper together without touching or getting out of their personal space. Be sure to call them into the space one at a time. Talk with students about how they feel when they have plenty of space, and how they feel when their personal space is invaded.

Question:

1. How can you appropriately ask for more space when it is needed?

(SECTION 5: SMALL GROUP ACTIVITIES AND LESSONS)

Happy Being Organized

GRADES: 1-5

 Objective: To have students practice listening and following directions to achieve the desired outcome.

Materials:
- 8 ½ x 11 white paper for each student
- Pencils
- Crayons

Directions:

1. Begin by asking the students what organization means. Make an "O" on a piece of paper while explaining that organization means listening and following directions. You stay organized in school when you listen and follow the directions given by adults. Also write an "L," "F," and "D" on the paper as you talk about this.

2. Tell the students that today they are going to practice listening and following directions by using only the letters "O," "L," "F," and "D."

3. Give each student a piece of paper and a pencil.

4. Help the students through these steps one by one while modeling it yourself.

    Fold your paper the "hamburger" (horizontal) way.

    Fold your paper the "hamburger" way again.

    Open your paper back out to reveal four boxes.

    Draw one big circle in the center, almost filling the page.

    On the fold line, draw a large "L."

108 | Youthlight, Inc. ©

Happy Being Organized, continued

At the edge of the circle, on the fold, draw a "D."

Turn your paper around to the opposite side and make another "D" on the edge of the circle at the fold.

Rotate your paper so it's the long way in front of you.

In the center of the upper right side of the circle, draw a "D."

In the center of the lower right side of the circle, draw a "D."

Put an "F" on top of each "D."

Put five "F's" on the far right side edge of the circle.

Now your drawing is complete, so draw a huge "C" for complete on the left side of the circle.

Turn your drawing around until you see a picture.

5. Show the picture on the following page so students can check to see how well they listened and followed directions.

6. If there is time remaining after the discussion questions below, students may color their pictures.

✳ Questions:

1. What picture do you see?
2. How do you feel when you listen and follow directions?
3. Why is organization important?

{SECTION 5: SMALL GROUP ACTIVITIES AND LESSONS}

Happy Being Organized

{SECTION 5: SMALL GROUP ACTIVITIES AND LESSONS}

Hands Up for Achievement

GRADES: 1-5

 Objective: To have students practice raising their hands to answer and ask questions.

Materials:
- "Hands Up" card
- Pencils

Directions:

1. Ask the students, "Who remembers how we show achievement in the classroom?" Explain how important it is for students to talk one at a time in a classroom so everyone can learn.

2. Encourage students to have fun interrupting as you ask the following questions.

    What school do you attend?

    Who is our school principal?

    What grade are you in?

    What is your favorite subject?

    What month is it?

    Who is the President of the United States?

    What would you like to ask me?

3. Explain to the students that you will ask the same questions again, but this time they will practice raising their hand and waiting to be called on before answering.

4. After discussing the questions below, give students a copy of the "Hands Up" card.

(SECTION 5: SMALL GROUP ACTIVITIES AND LESSONS)

Hands Up for Achievement, continued

5. Encourage students to keep the card in the corner of their desk at all times, and give themselves a check mark each time they raise their hand in class and have the correct answer. Ask students to bring their cards back to the next group meeting.

❋ Questions:

1. What happened when I asked the questions with lots of interrupting?

2. What happened when students raised their hands and waited?

3. Do you want students to demonstrate achievement in your classroom? Why or why not?

4. What should you do so all students can achieve in your classroom?

R is for Respect

Grades: 1-5

 Objective: To have students brainstorm the many different ways they can show respect.

Materials:
- Scrabble game letters

Directions:

1. Ask the students what respect in the classroom means. Respect in the classroom means being kind to others.

2. Brainstorm aloud with the students some of the many different ways to show respect. Examples: help, kind words, share, caring, listen, trust, take turns etc. (For 1st and 2nd grade students you will want to write the words as students share.)

3. Let the students help you spread the Scrabble letters out so they can all be seen.

4. Ask each student to find one word that means respect to them.

5. After each student has found one word, allow each student a turn to show their word and tell how it means respect.

6. Keeping the words they have already made; repeat the process. See how many of the letters can be used.

Questions:

1. How will you show respect in your classroom today?
2. How can you show respect at recess?
3. How can you show respect in the cafeteria?
4. What is a way to show respect this week that you haven't tried before?

(SECTION 5: SMALL GROUP ACTIVITIES AND LESSONS)

Teasing Isn't Cool

GRADES: K-5

✱ **Objective:** To teach students that it is not okay to tease or bully someone, and to give them strategies to use when someone teases them.

Materials:
- *Simon's Hook* by Karen Gedig Burnett, available through YouthLight, Inc.
- Toy fishing pole with fish
- Teasing statements written on index cards (you stink, four eyes, dum head, fish face, potty mouth, etc.)
- "No Teasing" contract on the following page.

Directions:
1. Ask students how they feel when they get teased. Explain to the students that if they give a strong reaction to the teaser, the teasing will continue. Tell students to listen for ways to discourage the teaser while you read *Simon's Hook*.

2. Discuss the questions listed below after reading the book.

3. Tape one of the index cards to the end of the fishing line. Give one child the pole, and another a fish. Have the students role play getting teased and effective ways to respond.

4. Students can sign the "no teasing" contract.

✱ Questions:

1. Is it okay to tease others? Why not?
2. What happens if you get mad when teased? Sad?
3. What can you do to discourage the teaser?
   Ignore   Change the subject   Walk away
   Laugh or make a joke   Avoid the teaser

I promise to stop teasing others.

If someone teases me, I will:

- Ignore the teaser by talking to a good friend.
- Walk away from the teaser and play with someone else.
- Choose to laugh or make a joke.
- Change the subject by asking a question about school work.
- Try to avoid the teaser in the future.

I promise to share this with my teacher and parents so they will know I am going to be a student that always shows RESPECT!

Student: _____

Teacher: _____

Parent: _____

{SECTION 5: SMALL GROUP ACTIVITIES AND LESSONS}

I'm Angry

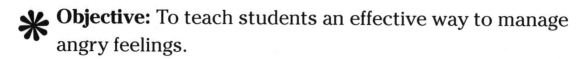

✱ Objective: To teach students an effective way to manage angry feelings.

Materials:
- Stop sign cards laminated and cut apart
- "I'm Angry" worksheets

Directions:

1. Explain that anger is an emotion we all have at times. Hand out the "I'm Angry" worksheets.

2. Ask students to read each situation and check off the ones that make them angry.

3. Discuss their answers by asking them questions like—How many of you checked off more than 2? More than 5? 8?

4. Tell the students that it is okay to be angry, but how we manage our angry feelings is very important. Even though we are angry, we have to keep our behavior under control.

5. Hand out the Stop sign cards to the students. Explain that picturing the Stop sign and quitting everything we are doing, helps us make good choices when we are angry. After we "Stop," we can count to ten, to calm down some so we can think about what to do.

6. Practice the situations on the "I'm Angry" worksheets, with each student touching the Stop sign and freezing, then counting to ten softly, and thinking of a good solution. Have students share their solutions.

7. Encourage the students to tape the Stop sign cards on their desks to remind them in class how to manage their anger.

{SECTION 5: SMALL GROUP ACTIVITIES AND LESSONS}

I'm Angry!

GRADES: K-5

Name _____

Put a check mark after each situation that makes you angry.

1. I forgot my lunch money. ____

2. A student is trying to copy my paper. ____

3. I can't read as well as the other kids. ____

4. My Math homework is too hard. ____

5. My brother tore a page out of my library book. ____

6. Someone keeps pushing me down at recess. ____

7. The teacher isn't calling on me when I raise my hand. ____

8. My pencil point keeps breaking. ____

9. My parents grounded me for a month. ____

10. I failed the Science test. ____

Total checks = ____

{SECTION 5: SMALL GROUP ACTIVITIES AND LESSONS}

I'm Angry!

Count to 10!

Count to 10!

Count to 10!

Count to 10!

Count to 10!

Count to 10!

{SECTION 5: SMALL GROUP ACTIVITIES AND LESSONS}

Let Go of Hurt

Objective: To teach students an effective way to share hurt feelings.

Materials:
- *The Hurt* by Teddi Doleski, available through Paulist Press
- "I-Message" worksheets duplicated for students
- Pencils
- Chart tablet or board

Directions:
1. Read *The Hurt* to the students.
2. After reading the book, ask the following questions.
   - What did Gabriel say when he got mad at Justin?
   - How did that make Justin feel? What did he do?
   - What did Justin do after his daddy stated that he was disappointed in him?
   - What happened to "The Hurt?"
   - After Justin finally shared his feelings with his daddy, how did he feel?
   - Now when Gabriel hurts Justin's feelings, what does Justin do?
3. Discuss the importance of always stating our feelings whenever we feel hurt.
4. Explain how to form an I-message. Write on the chart tablet—

   I feel _____ when you _____ because _____.

(SECTION 5: SMALL GROUP ACTIVITIES AND LESSONS)

Let Go of Hurt, continued

5. Give the students the following situations and ask them to state an I-message for each one.

- Someone took the only pencil off your desk. What could you say?

- Two of your friends are bossing you around at recess. What could you say?

- Someone always cuts in front of you in line. What could you say?

6. Ask the students to think of a problem situation they had recently with a friend.

7. Hand out the "I-message" sheets and have each student create an I-message to help with their problem.

8. Encourage the students to state the I-messages to their friends.

"I" Messages

I feel _____

when you _____

because _____

(SECTION 5: SMALL GROUP ACTIVITIES AND LESSONS)

Great Behavior = Great Friends

GRADES: 2-5

✸ **Objective:** To review what students have learned during the small group sessions on positive behavior.

Materials:
- "How to be a Great Friend!" worksheet
- Pencils

Directions:
1. Explain to the students that we will quickly review what they have learned during the group sessions (discuss questions below) and then they will complete a worksheet on their own.
2. Students complete the worksheet.
3. Review answers on the worksheet after all have finished.
4. Encourage students to take the worksheets home and share what they have learned with their parents.

✸ **Questions:**
1. How does keeping your hands and feet to yourself help you make friends?
2. If you listen when others are talking, does that help you have friends? Why or why not.
3. Name some different ways to show respect.
4. Is it okay to feel angry?
5. Name some things you should not do when you are angry.
6. Name some good things to do when angry.
7. Does keeping your anger under control help you to have more friends? Why or why not.
8. Explain how we worked as a team during our group sessions.

(SECTION 5: SMALL GROUP ACTIVITIES AND LESSONS)

Great Behavior = Great Friends

Name _____

✸ **Words to use: smile   listening   safe   help   kind   walk away**

I can show respect by always saying _____ words.

If someone teases me, I can _____.

When I keep my hands and feet to myself, everyone is _____.

If someone drops their books, I can _____ pick them up.

I can help us all learn and stay organized by _____.

Greet people with a big _____.

✸ **Fill in the blanks on your own. You can do it!**

Is it okay to feel angry? _____

Picture a _____ sign.

Count to _____.

Then, choose to _____ to someone about your feelings.

Say, "I feel _____ when you _____ because _____."

✸ **Draw a line to match the word with it's meaning.**

Share	When you and a friend want different things.
Take turns	The best way to work together.
Listen	When you and a friend need the same thing.
Patience	Pay attention to what a person says.
Team work	Calmly waiting your turn.

{SECTION 5: SMALL GROUP ACTIVITIES AND LESSONS}

Behavior to Flip Over

GRADES: K-5

 Objective: To have students practice handling difficult situations in a positive manner.

Materials:
- One quarter
- Situation cards duplicated and cut apart
- Stickers—happy face, stars (large enough to be noticed on a shirt)

Directions:
1. Explain that when students find themselves in a tough situation, sometimes they react poorly instead of using their "head" to think about how to handle the situation.

2. Tell the students they will take turns role playing how to make a good choice "using their head" in different situations.

3. Choose a student to flip the coin. If the student has "tails" he/she chooses a behavior card to read and then act out. If the student has "heads" he/she has to "use their head" to role play a positive behavior solution. The student who flipped the coin will choose another student to role play the other part.

4. Ask all students to watch the role play carefully and afterwards give a "thumbs up" or "thumbs down" to indicate how the student handled the difficult situation.

5. If the student received mostly "thumbs up," he/she gets a sticker to wear and chooses the student who will flip the coin next.

6. Repeat until all the students have had a chance to participate.

(SECTION 5: SMALL GROUP ACTIVITIES AND LESSONS)

Behavior to Flip Over, continued

1. How did you feel when students "used their head" to handle the situation?

2. Can you always make good choices for yourself? Why or why not?

Behavior to Flip Over, situation cards

A kid on the school bus calls you a name every day.	Your friend called to say she was going to go to someone else's house to play, when she had promised to come to your house.
Your little brother scribbled in your science textbook.	You keep raising your hand, but the teacher doesn't call on you.
A student pushes you on purpose as you get in line with the class.	A friend is using the red paint you need to finish a project, but he won't share.
You bring a basketball to use at recess, but someone grabs it from you as soon as you go outside.	Your mother promised to take you to a movie if you got an "A" in math, and now she has changed her mind.
Your father cancels your weekend visit with him. Now it's going to be a month before you see him.	The same student keeps asking to borrow a pencil and never gives it back.

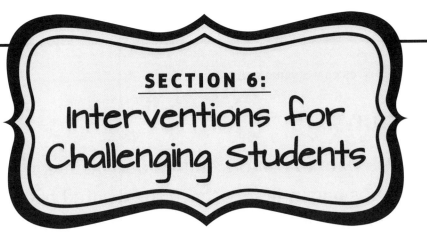

SECTION 6: Interventions for Challenging Students

Stay calm and remember that we all make mistakes.

(SECTION 6: INTERVENTIONS FOR CHALLENGING STUDENTS)

Interventions

✱ All students want to be noticed for good behavior. When those slip-ups occur; first re-teach the desired behavior. If after re-teaching, the undesirable behavior is still occurring, stay calm and remember that we all make mistakes. Try some of the intervention ideas below. Refrain from giving some meaningless punishment that has nothing to do with the misbehavior. No student likes to be embarrassed in front of the class.

More re-teaching: "I'm sorry but recess will be postponed today to give us extra time to practice _____. As soon as you show me you can _____, we'll all go outside."

Grandma's rule: "I understand you don't want to complete this work right now, but after you finish it, you can _____."

Re-direction: "Please show me what safety (organization, achievement, or respect) means in the classroom."

Notice the good: "Wow, I love how _____ (student's name) is showing us how to SOAR in the classroom. Let's see who else is SOARing." Call out the names of those students who corrected their behavior. "I like how _____ is SOARing too!

Encouragement: "I know this work is difficult for you, but I will help you until you understand."

Cool Down Corner: Have a special place where students can sit when they feel frustrated or angry. You need to model using this "spot" as well so students will be comfortable going there.

Cool Down Corner

Designate a place in the classroom where students may choose to sit when frustrated or mad. A desk and chair works best, but make sure the "spot" looks inviting. You do not want the student to feel like he/she is in "time out" or is being "punished" by choosing to sit there. You will need to set some simple rules with the students about when they can choose to sit there and how long they can stay.

Include the following items in the "Cool Down Corner:"

- Minute timer on top of desk
- Card taped to corner of desk with time reminder (5-10 minutes only)
- Picture of a STOP sign and reminder to count to 10.
- Squeeze ball or play dough inside desk
- Paper and pencil inside desk
- Small head pillow inside desk
- Chill Out Bag items (available through YouthLight, Inc.)

Instruct the students on how to utilize the "Cool Down Corner." It is best to model the use of the "spot" yourself.

Students need to learn to:

1. Sit quietly in chair or bean bag.
2. Set timer to not more than 10 minutes.
3. Choose how to calm down (squeeze ball, draw, or put head on pillow and count to 10).
4. Return to regular seat quietly.

Cool Down Corner

Cool Down Corner

#1: Set the timer for 5-10 minutes only!

#2: Make a calming choice—
  Count to 10 with head on pillow!
  Squeeze the ball.
  Draw a picture.
  Write about it!

#3: Return to my seat when I hear the ding!

{SECTION 6: INTERVENTIONS FOR CHALLENGING STUDENTS}

Bitter to Sweet

✽ All children, and adults, sometimes make poor choices. Teach students how to apologize by completing the form below. You can have the forms in the "Cool Down Corner" or use them to teach the entire class. Once students have apologized, you can look for opportunities for change in the future, and give an "oreo" as a reward.

I am sorry for _____.

Next time I will _____.

Please forgive me. I want to be your friend.

Individualized Behavior Plans

Most students will choose positive behavior after having been taught the school-wide expectations. About 10% of students need some additional attention, with lots of encouragement and rewards, to be able to choose positive behavior. For those students requiring additional encouragement and rewards, individualized behavior plans when implemented consistently, correct behavioral difficulties 99% of the time!

If a student is exhibiting inappropriate behavior, you first want to determine the positive behavior that is needed. For example blurting out in class is replaced with raising your hand to speak; getting out of seat is replaced with staying in seat. Instead of communicating what the student "should not" be doing; communicate what the student "should" be doing.

✱ **Communicate what the student "should" be doing.**

Once you define the behavior the student needs to demonstrate, you can then teach and "look" for this behavior to reward. It is important for the student to feel good about his/her behavioral improvement. When using an individualized behavior plan, start with a goal a bit more than half. Then increase the goal by a point or two as the student experiences success. One word of caution: Never set a goal as the total possible points; nobody is perfect!

{INDIVIDUALIZED BEHAVIOR PLANS}

Some guidelines for developing individualized behavior plans:

- Divide the student's daily schedule into segments.
- Choose the replacement behavior to reinforce (not more than two behaviors).
- Create a chart using this information.
- Choose the positive behavior picture cards on the following page that match the student's replacement behaviors.
- Recess works well as a mid-day reward.
- Figure total points for earning rewards. (Start small and increase the goal as student experiences success.)
- Decide on rewards.
- Keep behavior chart and positive behavior cards on student's desk.
- Keep a record of when the student meets his goal. (This is very helpful in determining how well the plan is working!)

Positive Behavior Picture Cards

Keep your hands, feet, and all objects to yourself. 	**Listen and follow directions.** 
Raise your hand to speak. 	**Be kind to others.** 
Speak kindly and quietly. 	**Do your best!** 

{INDIVIDUALIZED BEHAVIOR PLANS}

Younger Student Examples

_____'s Day   Date _____

❋ **Rule:** Listen to and follow directions.

Morning Work	**Reading**	**Writing**
Differentiated Instruction	**Recess** 4 = All recess 3 out of 4 = 15 min. 2 out of 4 = 10 min. 1 out of 4 = 5 min.	**Lunch**
Fine Arts	**Math**	**Science/S. Studi**
Goal = 5 out of 8 Total = _____	Positive comments: _____ _____ _____	Teacher signature: _____

Parent's signature _____

{INDIVIDUALIZED BEHAVIOR PLANS}

Name _____   Date _____

Schedule:	Time:	Complete Work:
☀	7:25- 8:00	
🌐	8:00-8:30	
🎨	8:30- 9:10	
ABC	9:10- 10:25	
🍎	10:25-10:55	
🛝	10:55-11:20	
📖	11:20-12:00	
45+7	12:00-1:00	
📝	1:00-1:30	
🧒	1:30-1:55	

Goal=7 out of 10

Parent's signature _____

{INDIVIDUALIZED BEHAVIOR PLANS}

SOAR – Make good choices and have a super day!

Name _____ Date _____

	Stay in my seat	Use kind words	Total
Morning Work			
Class Meeting			
Reading			
Fine Arts			
Math			
Lunch			
TOTAL			
Recess	9-12 = all recess	6-8 = 10 min. recess	3-5 = 5 min. recess
Writing			
SS/Science			
Differentiated Instruction			
10/18=reward			

Parent's signature _____

{INDIVIDUALIZED BEHAVIOR PLANS}

Older student examples

Name _____ Date _____

	Shows Respect	Completes Work
Review work		
Copy Homework		
Problem Solving		
Computer Lab		
Fine Arts		
Math		
Recess	8-12 all recess	7 or less—recess after work is completed
Phonics		
Writing		
Silent Reading		
Reading		
Pack-up		
TOTAL		

_____ can earn a total of 22 points.

_____ must have 15 points to earn a reward choice for the day.

Parent's signature _____

{INDIVIDUALIZED BEHAVIOR PLANS}

Name _____ Week of _____

SOARing Star		Monday	Tuesday	Wednesday	Thursday	Friday
7:05-7:45	Morning Time					
7:45-8:25	Fine Arts					
8:25-10:45	Reading					
10:45-11:20	Computer/Recess					
11:20-12:15	Math					
12:15-12:35	Lunch					
12:35-1:50	Science/S.S.					
1:50-2:10	Dismissal/CO					
Goal= ___ of 8						
Comments						

Rewards for Meeting Goal

Candy Jar

Happy Gram

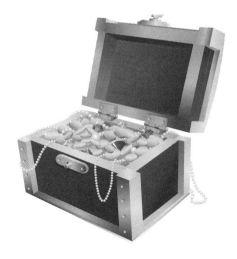

Treasure Chest

Good News Call

{INDIVIDUALIZED BEHAVIOR PLANS}

Behavior Tracking Form

_____ SOARS

Month ____	Monday	Tuesday	Wednesday	Thursday	Friday
Week of _____					

{INDIVIDUALIZED BEHAVIOR PLANS}

Remember — Be consistent! Think like a child!

When using behavior plans you must be committed to being consistent! The student needs feedback after <u>every</u> time or unit of study listed on their behavior chart.

If the student demonstrates the desired behavior during that time period, but the teacher fails to recognize that and give the student his/her earned point or sticker, the student may begin exhibiting poor behavior again. To the child, you didn't keep your promise of rewarding the desired behavior.

The converse is also true. If the child had difficulty showing you the desired behavior, and did not earn his/her point or sticker during the designated time period, and you say nothing, the child may think his/her behavior was okay. When the student does not demonstrate the desired behavior, you don't want to get in a long discussion. Just merely say (in private), "Johnny, you forgot to talk with respect during _____(time period). I know you can show respect during _____ (time period)."

{BEHAVIOR PLANS FOR HOME}

Behavior Plans for Home

Sometimes children will behave well at school, but misbehave at home. In fact, isn't it natural to demonstrate our best behavior when we are out in public; yet relax and show more of our true selves at home?

If a student is exhibiting inappropriate behavior at home, you first want to make sure you have rules in place which have been taught to your children. Once certain your child understands the rules at home, determine the positive behavior that is needed. For example refusing to complete homework is replaced with completing homework; a messy room is replaced with picking up toys. Instead of communicating what the student "should not" be doing; communicate what the student "should" be doing. Once you define the behavior the student needs to demonstrate, you can then teach and "look" for this behavior to reward. It is important for your child to feel good about his/her behavioral improvement. When using a behavior plan, start with a small, achievable goal. Then increase the goal by a day, after the child has been successful for a week or two. One word of caution: Never set a goal as the total possible; nobody is perfect!

Some guidelines for developing behavior plans at home:

- Divide the child's schedule into segments.
- Create a chart using this information.
- Figure total points for earning rewards. (Start small and increase goal as child experiences success.)
- Talk to your child and decide together on a list of possible daily rewards for meeting his/her goal.
- Keep a record of when your child meets his/her goal. (This is very helpful in determining how well the plan is working! It can be as simple as having the child put a sticker or happy face on your home calendar.)

{BEHAVIOR PLANS FOR HOME}

Young Child Example

	Sun.	Mon.	Tues.	Wed.	Thurs.	Fri.	Sat.
Dressed							
Teeth brushed							
Homework completed							
Room picked up							

Total= _____

Goal= _____ **out of 7 days**

✻ **Special notes:** Help your child check off all the chores as they are completed each day. At the end of the day, reward him/her with something free! (30 minutes of television, playing a game with the family, call a friend, 30 minutes of computer time, etc.)

Keep track of each day the chores are completed by allowing the child to put a sticker or special mark on the family calendar. At the end of the week, let the child choose something extra special, if for example he/she checked off all chores every day but 2 or 3. Agree in advance on weekend rewards (friend over, movie, picnic in park, etc.)

{BEHAVIOR PLANS FOR HOME}

Older Child Example

	Sun.	Mon.	Tues.	Wed.	Thurs.	Fri.	Sat.
Dressed and ready							
Bed made up							
Clothes in hamper							
Homework completed							
Room in order							
Trash taken out							

Total= _____

Goal= _____ **out of 7 days**

✱ **Special notes:** Older children will enjoy checking off all the chores as they are completed each day. At the end of the day, reward him/her with something free! (30 minutes of television, playing a game with the family, call a friend, 30 minutes of computer time, etc.)

Keep track of each day the chores are completed by allowing the child to put a sticker or special mark on the family calendar. At the end of the week, let the child choose something extra special, if for example he checked off all chores every day but 2 or 3. Agree in advance on weekend rewards (friend over, movie, picnic in park, etc.)

Resources & References

Albert, Linda (1996). *Cooperative Discipline.* Circle Pines, MN: American Guidance Service, Inc.

Bender, Janet M., Amy R. Murray (2003). *Perfect Pals, How to Juggle Your Way From Perfection to Excellence.* Chattanooga, TN: National Center for Youth Issues.

Burnett, Karen Gedig. (2000). *Simon's Hook: A Story About Teases and Put-downs.* Felton, CA: GR Publishing.

Cook, Julia (2006). *A Bad Case of Tattle Tongue.* Chattanooga, TN: National Center for Youth Issues.

Dinkmeyer, Don, Sr., Gary D. McKay, and Don Dinkmeyer, Jr. (1997). *The Parent's Handbook, Systematic Training for Effective Parenting.* Circle Pines, MN: American Guidance Service, Inc.

Doleski, Teddi (1983). *The Hurt.* Mahwah, NJ: Paulist Press.

Epstein, M., Atkins, M., Culliman, D., Kutash, K., and Weaver, R. (2008). *Reducing Behavior Problems in the Elementary School Classroom: A Practice Guide* (NCEE #2008-012). Washington, DC: National Center for Education Evaluation and Regional Assistance, Institute of Education Sciences, U.S. Department of Education. Retrieved from http://ies.ed.gov/ncee/wwc/publications/practiceguides.

Finnigan, Dave (1999). *Juggling for Success.* Atlanta, GA: Sportime International.

Lickona, Thomas (1992). *Educating for Character: How Our Schools Can Teach Respect and Responsibility.* New York, NY: Bantam Books.

Neiman, S. (2011). C*rime, Violence, Discipline, and Safety in U.S. Public Schools: Findings From the School Survey on Crime and Safety: 2009-10* (NCES 2011-320). U.S. Department of Education, National Center for Education Statistics. Washington, DC: U.S. Government Printing Office.

Nelsen, Jane (1987). Positive Discipline. New York, NY: Ballantine Books.

Nelsen, Jane, Linda Escobar, Katie Ortolano, Roslyn Duffy, and Deborah Owen-Sohocki (2001). Positive Discipline A Teacher's A-Z Guide, Rev. 2nd ed. New York, NY: Three Rivers Press.

Sugai, George, Robert Horner (2005) *School-wide Positive Behavior Support: Basics* Power Point, Center on Positive Behavioral Interventions and Supports, University of Oregon

Tobin, L. (1998). W*hat Do You Do With a Child Like This? Inside the Lives of Troubled Children.* Duluth, MN: Whole Person Associates.